www.ingramcontent.com/pod-product-compliance
Lightning Source LLC
Chambersburg PA
CBHW070830100426
4281JCB00003B/562

www.winthropfamily.org/books

LEARN

DEDICATION

To my family...

John Winthrop
March 2008

Wake up with a smile and go after life ... Live it, enjoy it, taste it, smell it, feel it.

JOE KNAPP

Hold fast the time! Guard it, watch it, every hour, every minute! Unregarded it slips away like a lizard, smooth, slippery, faithless. Hold every moment sacred. Give each clarity and meaning, each the weight of thine awareness, each its true and due fulfillment.

THOMAS MANN, Writer

The wise person possesses humility. He knows that his small island of knowledge is surrounded by a vast sea of the unkown.

HAROLD C. CHASE

Many people search blindly for the "meaning of life." What they don't seem to understand is that life does not have meaning through mere existence or acquisition or fun. The meaning of life is inherent in the connections we make to others through honor and obligation.

DR. LAURA SCHLESSINGER,
International radio host and author

Be kind, for everyone you meet is fighting a hard battle.
> PLATO, Philosopher & Educator

The great advantage of living in a large family is to learn about that early lesson of life's essential unfairness.
> NANCY MITFORD, The Pursuit of Love

There is no such thing in anyone's life as an unimportant day.
> ALEXANDER WOOLLCOTT

Happiness is a by-product of an effort to make someone else happy.
> GRETA BROOKER PALMER (1905-1953), Writer

There are two types of people – those who come into a room and say, "Well, here I am," and those who come in and say, "Ah, there you are."

FREDERICK COLLINS

You can easily judge the character of others by how they treat those who can do nothing for them or to them.

MALCOLM S. FORBES (1919-1990), Publisher

One of the most lasting pleasures you can experience is the feeling that comes over you when you genuinely forgive an enemy – whether he knows about it or not.

A. BATTISTA

The thing I hate about an argument is that it always interrupts a discussion.

G. K. CHESTERTON, Writer

The biggest threat to our well-being ... is the absence of moral clarity and purpose.
                                                RICK SHUMAN

Don't ever promise more than you can deliver, but always deliver more than you promise.
                                        LOU HOLTZ, Football Coach

Drive yourself to be punctual, and you will soon keep your appointments on time as naturally as you eat three times a day.
                            TED POLLOCK, Management Consultant

This is the true joy in life. The being used for a purpose recognized by yourself as a mighty one. The being a force of nature instead of a feverish, selfish little clod of ailments and grievances complaining that the world will not devote itself to making you happy.

I am of the opinion that my life belongs to the whole community, and as long as I live, it is my privilege to do for it whatever I can. I want to be thoroughly used up when I die. For the harder I work, the more I live. I rejoice in life for its own sake.

Life is no brief candle to me. It is a sort of splendid torch which I've got a hold of for a moment, and I want to make it burn as brightly as possible before handing it on to further generations.

GEORGE BERNARD SHAW

The man who has no imagination has no wings.
                                    MUHAMMAD ALI

Life is a great big canvas; throw all the paint on it you can.
                                    DANNY KAYE, Entertainer

Bargaining Tips:
- Be clear, in your own mind, about exactly what you're after.
- Do your homework, so that you are fully prepared to discuss every aspect and respond to every question and comment.
- Be persistent. Don't expect to "win" the first time. Your first job is just to start the other person thinking.
- Make friends with the person with whom you are bargaining. Put your bargain in terms of his or her needs, advantages, and benefits.
- Keep your sense of humor.

BENJAMIN FRANKLIN

ATTITUDE

The longer I live, the more I realize the impact of attitude upon life. Attitude, to me, is more important than facts. It is more important than the past, than education, than money, than circumstances, than failures, than successes, than what other people think or say or do. It is more important than appearance, giftedness or skill. It will make or break a company ... a church ... a home. The remarkable thing is we have a choice every day regarding the attitude we will embrace for that day. We cannot change our past ... we cannot change the fact that people will act in a certain way. We cannot change the inevitable. The only thing we can do is play on the one string we have, and that is our attitude ... I am convinced that life is 10% what happens to me and 90% how I react to it. And so it is with you ... we are in charge of our attitudes.

CHARLES SWINDOLL

The credit belongs to the man who is actually in the arena, whose face is marred by dust and sweat and blood ... who knows the great enthusiasms, the great devotions – and spends himself in a worthy cause – who at best if he wins, knows the thrills of high achievement – and if he fails, at least fails while daring greatly – so that his place shall never be with those cold and timid souls who know neither victory nor defeat.

PRESIDENT JOHN F. KENNEDY quoting
THEODORE ROOSEVELT December 9, 1961

Some think it's holding on that makes one strong; sometimes it's letting go.

SYLVIA ROBINSON

Success isn't permanent, and failure isn't fatal.

MIKE DITKA, Professional football coach

The closer one gets to the top, the more one finds there is no "top."

NANCY BARCUS

Gentility is what is left over from rich ancestors after the money is gone.

JOHN CIARDI, Poet

When we grow old, there can only be one regret; not to have given enough of ourselves.

ELEONORA DORA (1858-1924), Actress

ADVICE TO FRIENDS

- Your fences need to be horse-high, pig tight and bull-strong.
- Keep skunks, investment advisors and lawyers at a distance.
- Life is simpler when you plow around the difficulties.
- A bumble bee or a hornet is much faster than a tractor.
- Forgive your enemies – it messes up their heads.
- Do not corner something you know is meaner than you.
- It doesn't take a very big person to carry a grudge.
- Every path has a few puddles.
- The best sermons are lived, not preached.
- Most of the stuff people worry about isn't ever going to happen anyway.
- Don't judge folks by their relatives or their ancestors.
- Remember that silence is often the best answer.
- Live a good, honorable life. Then when you get older and think back, you'll enjoy it a second time.
- If you find yourself in a hole, the first thing you do is stop digging.
- The biggest troublemaker you'll probably ever have to deal with watches you from the mirror every morning.
- Always drink upstream from the herd.
- Letting the cat out of the bag is a whole lot easier than putting it back in.
- If you start to consider you're a person of some influence, try ordering somebody else's dog around.
- Live simply. Love generously. Care deeply. Speak kindly. And forgive everybody everything.
- Leave the rest to God.

AN AGING TREE FARMER

Forget.
Apologize.
Admit Errors.
Avoid mistakes.
Listen to advice.
Keep your temper.
Shoulder your blame.
Make the best of things.
Maintain high standards.
Think first and act accordingly.
Put the needs of others before your own.
Forgive.

Author Unknown

ANIMAL FACTS
- Giraffes can't swim.
- Hummingbirds can't walk.
- Sharks can't stay still.
- Whales can't swim backwards.
- Cats can't taste sugar.
- Tarantulas can survive 2.5 years without food.
- Dolphins sleep with one eye open.
- Snails can sleep for 3 years.
- Crocodiles swallow stones to help them dive deeper.
- Lobsters have blue blood.
- Grasshoppers have white blood.
- A chameleon's tongue is longer than its body.
- A Bloodhound's nose is admissible as evidence.
- Anteaters prefer termites.
- Squid can commit suicide by eating their own tentacles.

Author Unknown

MONEY...

It can buy you a house, but not a Home.
It can buy you a bed, but not Sleep.
It can buy you a clock, but not Time.
It can buy you a book, but not Knowledge.
It can buy you a position, but not Respect.
It can buy you medicine, but not Health.
It can buy you blood, but not Life.
It can buy you sex, but not Love.

So you see, money isn't everything. The best things in life can't be bought, and often we destroy ourselves trying.

I tell you all this because I am your friend, and as your friend I want to take away your needless pain and suffering...

So send me all your money and I will suffer for you. A truer friend than me you will never find.

Cash, personal checks or money orders are accepted.

Author Unknown

Can you imagine working at the following company?
It has a little over 500 employees with the following statistics:

- 29 have been accused of spousal abuse
- 7 have been arrested for fraud
- 19 have been accused of writing bad checks
- 117 have bankrupted at least two businesses
- 3 have been arrested for assault
- 71 cannot get a credit card due to bad credit ratings
- 14 have been arrested on drug-related charges
- 8 have been arrested for shoplifting
- 21 are current defendants in lawsuits
- 84 were stopped for drunk driving in 1998.

Can you guess what organization this is?

It is the 535 members of the United States Congress — the same group that perpetually cranks out hundreds of new laws designed to keep the rest of us in line.

Author Unknown, date unknown

WHO WOULD YOU CHOOSE? (true facts)

It's time to elect a world leader, and your vote counts. Here's the inside scoop on the three leading candidates. Choose wisely.

Candidate A:

consults with astrologists. He's had 2 mistresses. He chain-smokes and drinks 8 to 10 martinis a day.

Candidate B:

was kicked out of office twice, sleeps until noon, used opium in college and drinks a quart of brandy every day.

Candidate C:

is a decorated war hero. He's a vegetarian, doesn't smoke. Drinks an occasional beer and hasn't had any illicit affairs.

Which of these candidates is your choice?

Candidate A is Franklin D. Roosevelt. Candidate B is Winston Churchill. Candidate C is Adolph Hitler.

Author Unknown

Coincidence or history repeating itself?

Abraham Lincoln was elected to Congress in 1846.
John F. Kennedy was elected to Congress in 1946.

Abraham Lincoln was elected President in 1860.
John F. Kennedy was elected President in 1960.

The names Lincoln and Kennedy each contain seven letters. Both were particularly concerned with civil rights. Both wives became widows while living in the White House. Both Presidents were shot on a Friday. Both were shot in the head.

Here is an interesting one...
Lincoln's secretary was named Kennedy.
Kennedy's secretary was named Lincoln.

Both were assassinated by Southerners and were succeeded by Southerners. Both successors were named Johnson.

Andrew Johnson, who succeeded Lincoln, was born in 1808.
Lyndon Johnson, who succeeded Kennedy, was born in 1908.

John Wilkes Booth, who assassinated Lincoln, was born in 1839.
Lee Harvey Oswald, who assassinated Kennedy, was born in 1939

Both assassins were known by their three names. Both names comprise fifteen letters.

Booth ran from the theatre and was caught in a warehouse. Oswald ran from a warehouse and was caught in a theatre.

Booth and Oswald were assassinated before their trials.

And here is the kicker...
A week before Lincoln was shot, he was in Monroe, Maryland. A week before Kennedy was shot, he was in Marilyn Monroe.

Author Unknown

HOW MANY RELATIVES DO YOU HAVE?

Think you have enough to keep you busy? Let's see...

1 YOU
2 parents
4 grandparents
8 g grandparents
16 gg grandparents
32 ggg grandparents
64 gggg grandparents
128 ggggg grandparents
256 gggggg grandparents
512 ggggggg grandparents
1024 gggggggg grandparents
2048 ggggggggg grandparents
4096 gggggggggg grandparents
8192 ggggggggggg grandparents
16,184 gggggggggggg grandparents
32,768 ggggggggggggg grandparents
65,536 gggggggggggggg grandparents
131,072 ggggggggggggggg grandparents
262,144 gggggggggggggggg grandparents
524,288 ggggggggggggggggg grandparents
1,048,576 gggggggggggggggggg grandparents
2,097,152 ggggggggggggggggggg grandparents

Author Unknown

The World at a Glance

If the world was made up of only 100 people, there would be:

- 57 Asians
- 21 Europeans
- 14 from the Western Hemisphere (both North & South)
- 8 Africans
- 52 would be female
- 48 would be male
- 70 would be non-white 30 would be white
- 70 would be non-Christian 30 would be Christian
- 89 would be heterosexual 11 would be homosexual
- 6 people would possess 59% of the entire world's wealth, and all 6 would be from the United States
- 80 would live in substandard housing
- 70 would be unable to read
- 1 would be near death
- 1 would be near birth
- 1 (yes, only 1) would have a college education
- 1 would own a computer

Author Unknown, date unknown

LAUGH

COPYRIGHT © 2008 BY JOHN WINTHROP

None of the material contained herein is original. The joke and the quotes are merely a collection intended for the amusement and edi cation of the reader.

All rights reserved. No part of this publication may be reproduced, distributed, or transmitted in any form or by any means, including photocopying, recording, or other electronic or mechanical methods, without the prior written permission of the publisher, except in the case of brief quotations embodied in certain noncommercial uses permitted by copyright law.

Printed in the United States of America.

ISBN 978-0-9970242-1-0

J Winthrop, Charleston, South Carolina

www.winthropfamily.org

DEDICATION

To my helpers...
- in the office,
- at home,
- and elsewhere,
who have contributed to this random selection of jokes and quotes in so many ways to make life more productive and joyful.

John Winthrop
March 2008

STRESS DIET

Breakfast	1/2 grapefruit
	1 slice whole wheat toast 8 oz. skim milk
Lunch	4 oz. lean broiled chicken breast
	1 cup steamed zucchini
	1 Oreo cookie
	Herbal tea
Mid-Afternoon Snack	Rest of the package of Oreos
	1 quart Rocky Road Ice Cream
	1 jar hot fudge
Dinner	2 loaves garlic bread
	Large pepperoni & mushroom pizza
	Pitcher of beer
	3 Milky Way candy bars
	Entire frozen cheesecake eaten directly from freezer

Diet Tips

- If no one sees you eat it, it has no calories.
- If you drink a diet soda with a candy bar, they cancel each other out.
- When eating with someone else, calories don't count if you don't eat the same amount.
- Foods used for medicinal purposes NEVER count (such as hot chocolate brandy, toast with peanut butter, even Sara Lee Cheese Cake.)
- If you fatten up everyone else around you, then you look thinner.
- Movie-related foods don't count because they are simply part of the entertainment experience and not part of one's personal fuel, i.e. Milk Duds, popcorn with butter, Hershey bar with almonds.
- Cookie pieces contain no calories — the process of breakage causes caloric leakage.

Growing old is mandatory — growing up is optional.

Insanity is my only means of relaxation.

Forget the health food — I need all the preservatives I can get.

Blessed are those who hunger and thirst, for they are sticking to their diets.

You're getting old when you get the same sensation from a rocking chair that you once got from a roller coaster.

Perhaps you know why women over 50 don't have babies; they would put them down somewhere and forget where they left them.

My mind not only wanders, sometimes it leaves me completely.

Every time I think about exercise, I lie down until the thought goes away.

God put me on earth to accomplish a certain number of things. Right now I am so far behind, I will live forever.

It's frustrating when you know all the answers, but nobody bothers to ask you the questions. If you can remain calm, you just don't have all the facts.

Stress reducer: Put a bag on your head. Mark it "closed for remodeling." CAUTION: Leave air holes.

I finally got my head together and my body fell apart.

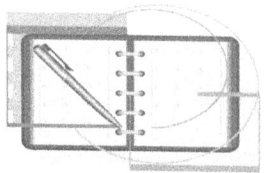

There cannot be a crisis this week; my schedule is already full.

The best way to forget all your troubles is to wear tight shoes.

50 Fun Things to Do in an Elevator

1. Make race car noises when anyone gets on or off.
2. Blow your nose and offer to show the contents of your Kleenex to other passengers.
3. Grimace painfully while smacking your forehead and muttering: "Shut up, damn-it, all of you just shut UP!"
4. Whistle the first seven notes of "It's a Small World" incessantly.
5. Sell Girl Scout cookies.
6. On a long ride, sway side to side at the natural frequency of the elevator.
7. Shave.
8. Crack open your briefcase or purse, and while peering inside ask: "Got enough air in there?"
9. Offer nametags to everyone getting on the elevator. Wear yours upside-down.
10. Stand silent and motionless in the corner, facing the wall, without getting off.
11. When arriving at your floor, grunt and strain to yank the doors open, then act embarrassed when they open by themselves.
12. Lean over to another passenger and whisper: "Noogie patrol coming!"
13. Greet everyone getting on the elevator with a warm handshake and ask them to call you Admiral.
14. One word: Flatulence!
15. On the highest floor, hold the door open and demand that it stay open until you hear the penny you dropped down the shaft go "plink" at the bottom.
16. Do Tai Chi exercises.
17. Stare, grinning at another passenger for a while, and then announce: "I've got new socks on!"
18. When at least 8 people have boarded, moan from the back: "Oh, not now, damn motion sickness!"
19. Give religious tracts to each passenger.
20. Meow occasionally.

(continued on next page)

21. Bet the other passengers you can fit a quarter in your nose.
22. Frown and mutter "gotta go, gotta go" then sigh and say "oops!"
23. Show other passengers a wound and ask if it looks infected.
24. Sing "Mary Had a Little Lamb" while continually pushing buttons.
25. Holler "Chutes away!" whenever the elevator descends.
26. Walk on with a cooler that says "human head" on the side.
27. Stare at another passenger for a while, then announce "You're one of THEM!" and move to the far corner of the elevator.
28. Burp, and then say "mmmm...tasty!"
29. Leave a box between the doors.
30. Ask each passenger getting on if you can push the button for them.
31. Wear a puppet on your hand and talk to other passengers "through" it.
32. Start a sing-along.
33. When the elevator is silent, look around and ask, "Is that your beeper?"
34. Play the harmonica.
35. Shadow box.
36. Say "Ding!" at each floor.
37. Lean against the button panel.
38. Say, "I wonder what all these do" and push the red buttons.
39. Listen to the elevator walls with a stethoscope.
40. Draw a little square on the floor with chalk and announce to the other passengers that this is your "personal space."
41. Bring a chair along.
42. Take a bite of a sandwich and ask another passenger: "Wanna see wha in muh mouf?"
43. Blow spit bubbles.
44. Pull your gum out of your mouth in long strings.
45. Announce in a demonic voice: "I must find a more suitable host body."
46. Carry a blanket and clutch it protectively.
47. Make explosion noises when anyone presses a button.
48. Wear "X-Ray Specs" and leer suggestively at other passengers.
49. Stare at your thumb and say, "I think it's getting larger."
50. If anyone brushes against you, recoil and holler "Bad touch!"

SEAT HOG

A man lay sprawled across three entire seats in a posh theatre. When the usher came by and noticed this, he whispered to the man, "Sorry, sir, but you're only allowed one seat."

The man groaned but didn't budge. The usher became impatient.

"Sir, if you don't get up from there I'm going to have to call the manager."

Again, the man just groaned, which infuriated the usher who turned and marched briskly back up the aisle in search of his manager. In a few moments, both returned and stood over the man. Together the two of them tried repeatedly to move him, but with no success. Finally, they summoned the police.

The cop surveyed the situation briefly then asked, "All right buddy, what's your name?"

"Sam," the man moaned.

"Where ya from, Sam?"

With pain in his voice, Sam replied, "The balcony."

DIARY OF A SOUTHERNER WHO MOVED NORTH

DEC 8, 5:00 PM: it's starting to snow. The first of the season and the first one we've seen in years. The wife and I took our hot buttered rums and sat by the picture window, watching the soft flakes drift down, clinging to the trees and covering the ground. It was beautiful!

DEC 9: We awoke to a lovely blanket of crystal white snow covering the landscape. What a fantastic sight! Every tree and shrub was covered with a beautiful white mantle. I shoveled snow for the first time in years and loved it. I did both our driveway and our sidewalk. Later a city snow plow came along and accidentally covered up our driveway with compacted snow from the street. The driver smiled and waved. I waved back and shoveled it again.

DEC 10: It snowed an additional 5 inches last night and the temperature dropped to around 11 degrees. Several limbs on the trees and shrubs snapped due to the weight of the snow. I shoveled our driveway again. Shortly afterwards the snowplow came by and did his trick again. Much of the snow is now brownish-gray.

DEC 11: Warmed up enough during the day to create some slush, which soon became ice when the temp dropped again. Bought snow tires for both cars. Fell on my rear in the driveway. $145 to a chiropractor, but nothing was broken. More snow and ice expected.

DEC 12: Still cold. Sold the wife's car and bought a jeep with snow tires in order to get her to work. Slid into a guardrail anyway and did a considerable amount of damage to the right rear quarter-panel. Had another 8 inches of the white stuff last night. Both vehicles covered in salt and crud. More shoveling in store for me today. That godawful snow plow came by twice today!

DEC 13: Two degrees outside. More of that awful snow. Not a tree or shrub on our property that hasn't been damaged. Power was off most of the night. Tried to keep from freezing to death with candles and a kerosene heater, which tipped over and nearly burned the house down. I managed to put the flames out, but suffered second-degree burns on my hands and lost all my eyelashes and eyebrows. Car slid on ice on way to emergency room and was totaled.

DEC 14: Snow keeps on coming down. Have to put on all the clothes we own just to get to the mailbox. If I ever catch the slob that drives that snow plow I'll chew open his chest and rip out his heart. I think he hides around the corner and waits for me to finish shoveling and then comes down the street about 100 mph and buries our driveway again. Power still off. Toilet froze. Part of the roof has started to cave in.

DEC 15: Another foot of snow and sleet and ice, God knows what other kind of stuff fell last night. I wounded the driver of the snowplow with an ice ax, but he got away. Wife left me. Car won't start. I think I'm going snow-blind. I can't move my toes. Haven't seen the sun in weeks. More snow is forecast for the weekend. I think it's time to move back to South Carolina.

PLAY ON WORDS

Two antennas meet on a roof, fall in love and get married. The ceremony wasn't much, but the reception was excellent.

Two hydrogen atoms walk into a bar. One says, "I've lost my electron." The other says, "Are you sure?" The first replies, "Yes, I'm positive."

Two peanuts walk into a bar, and one was a salted.

A sandwich walks into a bar. The bartender says, "Sorry, we don't serve food in here."

A man walks into a bar with a slab of asphalt under his arm and says, "A beer please, and one for the road."

Two cannibals are eating a clown. One says to the other, "Does this taste funny to you?"

Two cows standing next to each other in a pasture. Daisy says to Dolly, "I was artificially inseminated this morning." "I don't believe you," says Dolly. "It's true, no bull!" exclaimed Daisy.

An invisible man marries an invisible woman. Their kids were nothing to look at either.

A man takes his Rottweiler to the vet and says, "My dog's cross-eyed. Is there anything you can do for him?" "Well," says the vet, "let's have a look at him." So he picks the dog up and examines his eyes. Finally, he says, "I'm going to have to put him down." "What? Because he's cross-eyed?" "No, because he's really heavy."

A man went to buy some camouflage trousers but couldn't find any.

I went to the butcher's the other day and I bet him 50 bucks that he couldn't reach the meat off the top shelf. He said, "No, the steaks are too high."

What do you call a fish with no eyes? A fsh.

AN ENGINEER'S VIEW OF SANTA CLAUS

No known species of reindeer can fly. But there are 300,000 species of living organisms yet to be classified, and while most of these are insects and germs, this does not completely rule out flying reindeer which only Santa has ever seen.

There are 2 billion children (persons tinder 18) in the world. But since Santa doesn't (appear to) handle the Muslim, Hindu, Jewish and Buddhist children, that reduces the workload to about 15% of the total - 378 million according to the Population Reference Bureau. At an average (census) rate of 3.5 children per household, that is 91.8 million homes. One presumes there's at least one good child in each.

Santa has 31 hours of Christmas to work with, thanks to the different time zones and the rotation of the earth, assuming he travels east to west (which seems logical). This works out to 822.6 visits per second. This is to say that for each Christian household with good children, Santa has 1/1000'h of a second to park, hop out of the sleigh, jump down the chimney, fill the stockings, distribute the remaining presents under the tree, eat whatever snacks have been left, get back up the chimney and into the sleigh, and move on to the next house.

Assuming that each of these 91.8 million stops are evenly distributed around the earth (which, of course, we know to be false but for the purposes of our calculation we will accept), we are now talking about 0.78 miles per household, a total trip of 71.6 million miles, not counting stops to do what most of us must do at least once every 31 hours, plus feeding, etc.. This means that Santa's sleigh is moving at 650 miles per second, or 3,000 times the speed of sound. For purposes of comparison, the fastest man-made vehicle on earth, the Ulysses space probe, moves at a pokey 27.4

(continued on next page)

miles per second, while a conventional reindeer can run, tops, at 15 miles per hour.

The payload on the sleigh adds another interesting element. Assuming that each child gets nothing more than a medium-size Lego set (2 pounds), the sleigh is carrying 321,300 tons, not counting Santa, who is invariably described as overweight. On land, conventional reindeer can pull no more than 300 pounds. Even granting that "flying reindeer" (see point #1) pull ten times the normal amount, we cannot do the job with eight, or even nine. We need 214,200 reindeer. This increases the payload to 353,430 tons; for comparison, this is four times the weight of the Queen Elizabeth.

353,430 tons traveling at 650 miles per second creates enormous air resistance - This will heat the reindeer up in the same fashion as a spacecraft re-entering the earth's atmosphere. The lead pair of reindeer will absorb 14.3 quintillion joules of energy per second each. In short, they will burst into flame instantaneously, exposing the reindeer behind them, and create a deafening sonic boom in their wake. The entire reindeer team will be vaporized within 4.26 thousands of a second. Santa, meanwhile, will be subjected to centrifugal forces 17,500 times greater than gravity. A 250-pound Santa (which seems ludicrously slim) would be pinned to the back of his sleigh by 4,315,015 pounds of force.

In conclusion, if Santa ever did deliver presents on Christmas Eve, he's been vaporized by now. The moral of this analytical essay, especially for young readers, is that you never should believe everything you read.

HOW TO BATHE A CAT

Thoroughly clean toilet.

Lift both lids and add shampoo.

Find and soothe cat as you carry him to the bathroom.

In one swift move, place cat in toilet, close both lids and stand on top so cat cannot escape.

The cat will self agitate and produce ample suds. (Ignore ruckus inside toilet; The cat is enjoying this.)

Flush toilet 3 or 4 times. This provides power rinse, which is quite effective.

Have someone open outside door, stand as far from the toilet as possible and quickly lift both lids.

Clean cat will rocket out of the toilet and outdoors, where he will air dry.

Sincerely,

The Dog

WORKSHOPS...

SELF-IMPROVEMENT WORKSHOPS
- Creative Suffering
- Overcoming Peace of Mind
- You and Your Birthmark
- Guilt Without Sex
- The Primal Shrug
- Ego Gratification Through Violence
- Holding Your Child's Attention Through Guilt and Fear
- Dealing With Post Self-Realization Depression
- Whine Your Way to Alienation
- How to Overcome Self-Doubt Through Pretense and Ostentation

BUSINESS/CAREER WORKSHOPS
- Money Can Make You Rich
- Talking Good: How You Can Improve Speech and Get a Better Job
- How I Made $100 in Real Estate
- Packaging and Selling Your Child: Parents Guide to the Porn Market
- Career Opportunities in Iran
- How to Profit From Your Own Body
- Underachievers Guide to Very Small Business Opportunities
- Filler Phrases for Thesis Writers
- Tax Shelters for the Indigent
- Looter's Guide to America's Cities

HOME ECONOMICS WORKSHOPS
- How You Can Convert Your Family Room Into a Garage
- How to Cultivate Viruses in Your Refrigerator
- Burglar-Proof Your Home With Concrete
- Basic Kitchen Taxidermy
- Sinus Drainage at Home
- 101 Other Uses For Your Vacuum Cleaner
- The Repair and Maintenance of Your Virginity
- How to Convert a Wheelchair into a Dune Buggy
- What To Do With Your Conversation Pit
- Christianity and the Art of RV Maintenance

HEALTH AND FITNESS WORKSHOPS
- Tap Dance Your Way to Social Ridicule
- Optional Body Functions
- Creative Tooth Decay
- Exorcism and Acne
- The Joys of Hypochondria
- High Fiber Sex
- Suicide and Your Health
- Bio-feedback and How To Stop It
- Skate Your Way to Regularity
- Understanding Nudity

CRAFTS WORKSHOPS
- Self-Actualization Through Macramé
- Needlecraft for Junkies
- Northern New Mexico Guide to Bad Taste Cuticle Crafts
- Mobiles and Collages With Fetishes
- Gifts for the Senile
- Bonsai Your Pet

MR. & MRS. POTATO

You know that all potatoes have eyes. Well, Mr. and Mrs. Potato had eyes for each other and they finally got married and had a little one - a real SWEET POTATO whom they called "YAM". They wanted the best for little Yam, telling her all about the facts of life. They warned her about going out and getting half baked because she could get Mashed, get a bad name like Hot Potato, and then end up with a bunch of Tater Tots.

She said not to worry -- no Mr. McSpud would get her in the sack and make a Rotten Potato out of her! But she couldn't stay home and become a Couch Potato either. She would get plenty of food and exercise so as not to be skinny like her Shoestring cousins.

Mr. and Mrs. Potato even told her about going off to Europe and to watch out for the Hard Boiled guys from Ireland and even the greasy guys from France called the French Fries. They also said she should watch out for the Indians when going out west because she could get Scalloped.

She told them she would stay on the straight and narrow and wouldn't associate with those high class Blue Belles or the ones from the other side of the tracks who advertise their trades on all the trucks you see around town that say Frito-Lay.

Mr. & Mrs. Potato wanted the best for Yam, so they sent her to 'Idaho U." - that's Potato University - where the Big Potatoes come from and when she graduated, she'd really be in the Chips. But one day she came home and said she was going to marry Walter Cronkite. Mr. & Mrs. Potato were very upset and begged Yam not to marry him, because   after all ... he's just a COMMON TATER!

CHILDREN'S BOOKS THAT NEVER MADE IT

- You Are Different and That's Bad
- The Boy Who Died From Eating All His Vegetables
- Dad's New Wife Robert
- Fun four-letter Words to Know and Share
- Hammers, Screwdrivers and Scissors: An I-Can-Do-It Book
- The Kids' Guide to Hitchhiking
- Kathy Was So Bad Her Mom Stopped Loving Her
- Curious George and the High-Voltage Fence
- All Cats Go to Hell
- The Little Sissy Who Snitched
- Some Kittens Can Fly
- That's It: I'm Putting You Up for Adoption
- Grandpa Gets a Casket
- The Magic World Inside the Abandoned Refrigerator
- Garfield Gets Feline Leukemia
- The Pop-Up Book of Human Anatomy
- Strangers Have the Best Candy
- Whining, Kicking and Crying to Get Your Way
- You Were an Accident
- Things Rich Kids Have, But You Never Will
- Pop! Goes The Hamster ...And Other Great Microwave Games
- The Man in the Moon is Actually Satan
- Your Nightmares Are Real
- Where Would You Like to Be Buried?
- Eggs, Toilet Paper, and Your School
- Why Can't Mr. Fork and Ms. Electrical Outlet Be Friends?
- Places Where Mommy and Daddy Hide Neat Things
- Daddy Drinks Because You Cry

Memorandum
To: Speculators
From: Charleston - based Venture Capitalist (JW)

While I do not have a great deal of expertise in the investment field, I do believe I have come across an excellent opportunity, which you may wish to consider for your own portfolio or for one or two of your best individual clients. I think we are probably looking at a possible limited partnership at this point.

Since the signing of NAFTA there has been a quiet, but rapid expansion of American investment in Mexican cat ranches. I first read about these in Money magazine, and later learned more from friends on Wall Street who believe this emerging industry has great profit potential for a minimum of risk.

I have learned that one of these ranches is about to come on the market near the town of Hermosille about 600 miles south of Mexico City. An option on it can be secured before word of its availability even gets out.

I would suggest we start relatively small with around a million cats. Each cat averages twelve kittens a year, so at a minimum we are talking about 12 million animals a year. Currently the white pelts go for $.20 a piece, while high quality black, silky ones go for as much as twice that. You'd think the white ones would be more expensive. Not so.

You can do the math yourself, but basically we are looking at gross income of $3,000,000 the first year alone. Excluding Sundays and official Mexican holidays, this works out to $10,000 a day.

I am told that a good Mexican cat man can skin about 50 cats per day at a wage of $3.15 an hour. Figuring that we will have to employ 663 "skinners" six-days-a-week, we are looking at a net profit of $8,200 per day (not including NAFTA tax credits).

A key to the whole business is that cats be fed exclusively rats. Rats multiply four times as fast as cats. We'll probably have to buy some land adjacent to the cat ranch to support a rat farm of, say, one million rats. This works out to four rats per cat each day - a virtual feast for the average feline!

Now, here's a marvelous twist to the whole deal. We feed the cat carcasses to the rats. This gives each rat one-quarter of a skinned cat. You don't need to calculate to see the beauty of this self-sustaining operation. The cats get the rats; the rats get the carcasses - and we're laughing all the way to the bank with 12 million pelts.

I hope you are sitting down. I am told that a California biotech firm is working on a technique to genetically cross cats with snakes. This means the cats will be able to shed their own pelts twice a year - giving us two skins instead of one! It would completely eliminate our labor costs. You and I would have to make a couple of trips to Hermosille each year to collect them, but if we brought other family members, it would only take a day or two. It would also be a nice way for us to have an extended family reunion at a future date.

Of course, we could write off the entire cost of the trip as well.

Do not, under any circumstances, mention this to anyone you work with in New York. The last thing we need is some hot shot, big money types homing in on this market and driving up costs for everyone.

I've even thought of a couple of names - "Fluffy Farms" or "Happy Tails" Ranch. Maybe we could do a logo with a bunch of smiling cat faces with the individual letters spelled across their teeth.

As a financial expert, I'd like to know your thoughts.

 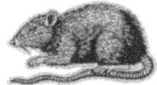

THE REVEREND CALVERT FITZGERALD
Rescue Mission
714 Bowery
New York, N.Y.

May 10, 1993

Dear Friend:

Perhaps you have heard of me and my nation-wide campaign in the cause of abstinence. Each year for the past 14 years, I have made a tour of the country and delivered a series of lectures on the evils of wenching.

On these tours, I have been accompanied by a young man, friend, and assistant, Clyde Lindstrom; Clyde is a pathetic case, a young man of good family and excellent background whose life was ruined by excessive indulgence in sex, late hours, and some drinking, not to mention various media of pornography.

Clyde would appear with me at lectures and sit on the platform drooling at the mouth and staring at the audience through bloodshot eyes while I would point him out as an example of what such a life would do.

Last summer during a fit of heavy breathing, Clyde died. A mutual friend has given me your name, and I wonder if you would care to accompany me on the tour this summer and take poor Clyde's place.

Yours sincerely,

Rev. Calvert Fitzgerald

10 TACTFUL WAYS TO EXPRESS LACK OF BRILLIANCE...

- The wheel's spinning, but the hamster's dead.
- Doesn't have all his dogs on one leash.
- Doesn't know much but leads the league in nostril hair.
- Dumber than a box of hair.
- All foam, no beer.
- As smart as bait.
- His belt doesn't go through all the loops.
- No grain in the silo.
- Lights on; no one' home.
- He's not the sharpest knife in the drawer.

THINGS YOU DON'T WANT TO HEAR DURING SURGERY

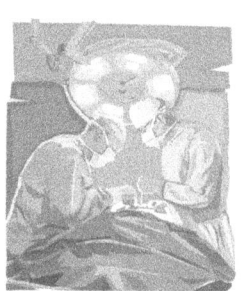

- "Better save that. We'll need it for the autopsy."
- "Someone call the janitor-we're going to need a mop."
- "Wait a minute. If this is his spleen, then what's that?"
- "Could you stop that thing from beeping - it's throwing my concentration off."
- "Oops! Has anyone ever survived 500 mls. of this stuff before?"
- "On no! I just lost my Rolex!"
- "I hate it when they're missing stuff in here."
- "That's cool! Now can you make his leg twitch?"
- "I wish I hadn't forgotten my glasses."
- "Hand me that...uh...that uh...thingie."
- "What's this doing here?"
- "Everyone stand back! My contact lens is in there somewhere!"
- "Well, folks, this will be an experiment for all of us."
- "Sterile, schmerile. The floor's clean, right?"
- "Nurse, did this patient sign the organ donor card?"
- "Don't worry. I think it's sharp enough."
- "Oh No! Page 47 of the manual is missing!"
- "Rufus! Comeback with that! Bad dog!"
- "She's gonna blow! Everyone take cover!"
- "Anyone seen where I left that scalpel?"
- "Ok-Now take a picture from this angle. This is truly a freak of nature."
- "FIRE! FIRE! Everyone get out!"

TEN ACTUAL LETTERS FROM CHILDREN TO GOD ...

I bet it is very hard for you to love all of everybody in the whole world. There are only four people in our family and I can never do it. Nan If you watch the church on Sunday I will show you my new shoes. Mickey I would like to live 900 years like that guy in the Bible.
    Love, Chris

We read Thomas Edison made light. But in Sunday School they said you did it. So I bet he stole your idea.
    Sincerely, Donna

It is great the way you always get the stars in the right places.
    Jeff

The bad people laughed at Noah -- you made an ark on dry land. But he stuck with you. That's what I would do.
    Eddie

I do not think anybody could be a better God. Well I just want you to know but I am not just saying that because you are God.
    Charles

I didn't think orange went with purple until I saw the sunset you made on Tuesday. That was cool.
    Eugene

I am doing the best I can.
    Frank

CONTINUE READING... FLIP BOOK OVER TO LEARN

CONTINUE READING... FLIP BOOK OVER FOR SOME LAUGHS

www.winthropfamily.org/books